SandCastle™

Science Made Simple

She'll Use a Ruler So You Won't Fool Her!

Kelly Doudna

Consulting Editors, Diane Craig, M.A./Reading Specialist
and Susan Kosel, M.A. Education

Published by ABDO Publishing Company, 4940 Viking Drive, Edina, Minnesota 55435.

Printed in the United States.

Credits
Edited by: Pam Price
Curriculum Coordinator: Nancy Tuminelly
Cover and Interior Design and Production: Mighty Media
Photo Credits: Brand X Pictures, Digital Vision, Kelly Doudna, Photodisc, ShutterStock, Wewerka Photography

Library of Congress Cataloging-in-Publication Data

Doudna, Kelly, 1963-
      She'll use a ruler so you won't fool her! / Kelly Doudna.
        p. cm. -- (Science made simple)
      ISBN 10 1-59928-618-1 (hardcover)
      ISBN 10 1-59928-619-X (paperback)

      ISBN 13 978-1-59928-618-1 (hardcover)
      ISBN 13 978-1-59928-619-8 (paperback)
      1. Length measurement--Juvenile literature. 2. Rulers (Instruments)--Juvenile literature. I. Title.
   II. Series: Science made simple (ABDO Publishing Company)

QC102.D68 2007
516'.15--dc22   2006015235

SandCastle Level: Transitional

SandCastle™ books are created by a professional team of educators, reading specialists, and content developers around five essential components—phonemic awareness, phonics, vocabulary, text comprehension, and fluency—to assist young readers as they develop reading skills and strategies and increase their general knowledge. All books are written, reviewed, and leveled for guided reading, early reading intervention, and Accelerated Reader® programs for use in shared, guided, and independent reading and writing activities to support a balanced approach to literacy instruction. The SandCastle™ series has four levels that correspond to early literacy development. The levels help teachers and parents select appropriate books for young readers.

Emerging Readers
(no flags)

Beginning Readers
(1 flag)

Transitional Readers
(2 flags)

Fluent Readers
(3 flags)

These levels are meant only as a guide. All levels are subject to change.

A **ruler** is a tool for measuring length in inches or centimeters. A **yardstick** shows length in inches. A **meterstick** shows length in centimeters.

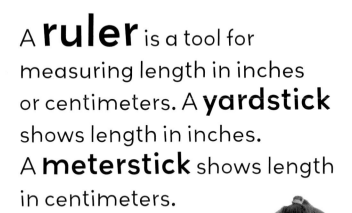

Words used to talk about rulers:

inch	length
centimeter	long
height	measure

I use one side of the ruler to measure the length of a in inches.

I use the other side of the ruler to measure the length of a in centimeters.

A ruler shows me

that my ——————

is 6 inches long.

A ruler shows me that my is 10 centimeters long.

A yardstick tells me

how long the

is in inches.

A meterstick tells me how long the is in centimeters.

She'll Use a Ruler So You Won't Fool Her!

Here is a girl named Bree
who has planted a tree.
She wants to measure
her leafy treasure.

I'll put the zero end
of my yardstick down
so that it touches
the ground.

Bree looks on her yardstick
for the nearest inch tick.
She can see that the tree
goes up to twenty-three.

Let me be brief,
I measured
the highest leaf.

Bree knows it
would be neater
to measure by centimeter.
Her meterstick shows 58,
and Bree thinks
that's just great!

I won't tell any lies,
I've seen it with
my own eyes!

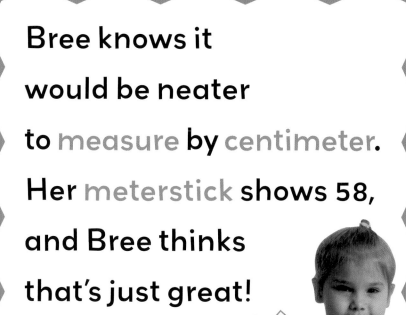

We Use
a Ruler
Every Day!

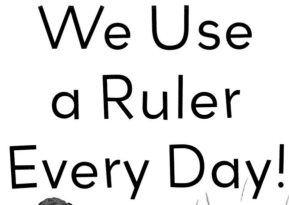

Jenny and Katie went fishing. They caught a big fish.

Jenny and Katie used a yardstick to find out that their fish is 20 inches long.

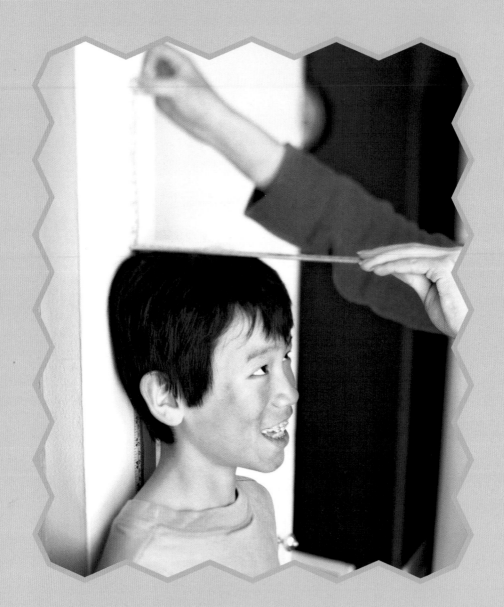

18

Ken's mother marks his height on the wall. She wants to know how tall Ken has grown.

Ken's mother uses a measuring tape to measure how many inches it is from the floor to the mark.

Linda will use a ruler to measure the dandelions she picked.

Linda wants to know how many centimeters long each one is.

Lola and Juan will use a ruler to measure Juan's shoe.

What things could you measure with a ruler?

Glossary

brief – short in time or length.

centimeter – a unit of length in the metric system of measurement. There are 100 centimeters in 1 meter.

inch – a unit of length in the U.S. customary system of measurement. There are 36 inches in 1 yard.

tick – a small line or spot that marks units of measurement on a ruler or scale.